"Koraly Dimitriadis is a poet of the finest balance. She writes with the tenderness of a loving hand and a fist that smashes oppression."
– Tony Birch, bestselling author, *White Girl,* and Boisbouvier Chair in Australian Literature

"One poem might punch you in the balls where another leaves you trying to collect shattered pieces from a foetal position in the corner … a voice that literally demands to be heard."
– *Overland Literary Journal*

"*Love and Fuck Poems* is raw, audacious and courageous. Bravo!"
– Christos Tsiolkas, bestselling author, *The Slap*

"Blood, Fire, Love & I
– TT.O., award winni

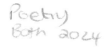

"A gutsy, defiant firec□   be
read angrily out loud □   ned
poetic celebration of   of
marital convention, sexual repression, and cultural obligation."
– Maxine Beneba Clarke, award-winning author, *The Hate Race*

"This is the sort of poetry we need. It has a love of the resonance of words, but most importantly, huge courage and surprising insight. Provocative, sure, but not provocation purely for its own sake – Dimitriadis' poems are explosively political and humane."
– Andy Jackson, award-winning poet, *Human Looking*

"Koraly writes in a voice that you need to hear. Her pride and passion is powerful, vulnerable, tentative, strong. The way she fucks with our sense of φιλότιμο – pride – will be chillingly resonant and painfully desirable to women from our community who have refused themselves a voice."
– Esther Anatolitis, editor, *Meanjin Literary Journal*

"Relentlessly bold, unapologetic, and humorous at all the right times. If one can detect a new wave of Australian poetry on the rise, it's due in no small part to the pioneering efforts of Koraly Dimitriadis."
– Ruby Hamad, author, *White Tears, Brown Scars*

Also by Koraly Dimitriadis

Just Give Me the Pills
She's Not Normal

Love & f♥ck poems

Koraly Dimitriadis

the anniversary edition

press

outside the box

First published in 2012
Reprinted in 2013, 2014, 2016
Translated into Greek in 2014, republished 2016

Outside The Box Press
www.outsidetheboxpress.com

ISBN 978-0-9872777-6-3

ISBN 978-0-9872777-7-0 (e-book)
ISBN 978-0-646564-21-0 (original zine)
ISBN 978-0-9872777-0-1 (deluxe edition)
ISBN 978-0-9930174-3-8 (honest publishing uk edition)
ISBN 978-9963-2882-1-2 (astaman cyprus greek edition)
ISBN 978-0-9930174-9-0 (honest publishing uk greek edition)

Cover image by Kaliopi Malamas
Cover design by Rosie G and Ilura Design

Author photograph by Nicholas Purcell, 2009

Typeset by Ilura Design
www.ilurapress.com

A catalogue record for this
book is available from the
NATIONAL LIBRARY OF AUSTRALIA
National Library of Australia

For Anna Kannava:
'Gorgeous, don't listen to anyone
just write what you like …
and as long as you're
having some sex, darling …'

Preface

Since releasing the zine in 2011, *Love and Fuck Poems* has taken me on an exciting journey where I have learned a lot, both personally and professionally. Today, I look back on these poems with a fondness and humour – there are elements of me still here, but I have moved on from this chapter of my life. Readers can see my evolution in *Just Give Me The Pills,* and in forthcoming poetry books *She's Not Normal, Hazardously Searching For Mr Right,* and in my first non-fiction book, *Not Till You're Married.*

Apart from celebrating the ten-year milestone, I am re-releasing *Love and Fuck Poems* firstly to incorporate my original zine drawings. I wanted to do this initially, but I thought 'the industry' wouldn't take me seriously if I did. Since then, many poets have incorporated drawings with huge success, so I'm embracing my little drawings now. I've included one extra poem 'The Queen', which was written around the same time *Love and Fuck Poems* was. The acknowledgements are as they were in 2012.

Secondly, I want to cast a wider and smarter net with my distribution, as when I first released it, I didn't know much about book distribution. For example, when I first published I had very positive reviews on Amazon. But then suddenly, my book was stripped of all its reviews and buried in their dungeon, with no explanation other than I had breached community standards. My attempts for an explanation were futile. Books in the dungeon are not visible in general searches, you can only find them searching by their name.

Today, we have many books with 'fuck' in the title, like *The Subtle Art of Not Giving a Fuck,* and *Go The Fuck To Sleep,* but back when I launched there were none in the mainstream. Also, when we first printed the book we were concerned about customs in China not allowing copies to be shipped to Australia, but were surprised when they were stopped by Australian customs for pornographic content.

I have always seen my book as feminist literature. It's interesting, when a man writes a book with 'fuck' in the title, it is splashed all over the world, but when a woman writes about reclaiming her body, her book is stripped of its acclaim and buried in a dungeon.

Let's see how the anniversary edition goes.

Volcano

You say I'm like a volcano
spurting my poetry like magma,
but there's one point you overlooked
as you held me naked in the night

It is impossible to live inside a volcano
You cannot stand beside one
And any villages nearby
are obliterated by eruptions.
Red-tempered, unapologetic
a volcano shows no mercy
naturally covering and re-covering
its surrounds in boiling rock liquid

There's one point you overlooked
as you fought me naked in the night

Nobody is crazy enough
To go near a volcano
And the ones that do
Never survive long

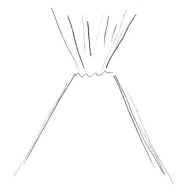

Define me

square me.
stake the fence,
high.

bless me,
with golden
chimes

pray for my soul.
pray.

bake me,
Greek pastries.
smash 'em with my fist.
splat.

keep me,
a show prize.
hook,
catch on that barbed wire.

watch me.
watch me ignite,
burn.

shove me,
to the altar:
throw confetti.
watch it fall

lock me
go ahead
lock me
in a box
lock me

smell me.
is that sex you smell?
(don't confuse yourself)

define me.
go ahead.
define me.

Canadian ice-skater

From a box of flicker
you appear before me.
Lyrically you glide,
along expanses of ice.
Classically you dance
in her arms – to my rhythm.

Fill me with Canadian pride
just to taste a drop of your red wine
and roll in fluffs of your white snow.
Promise me Olympic rings
amongst rocky mountains
and wet maple leaves.

Promise.

I can't look.

I can't look at you Canadian ice-skater
yet my gaze lifts and sticks
my teeth grind on your ice –
Dance with her, go on, dance,
razor skate over my flesh
to win that gold medal.

Sacrifice yourself.
Go on.
Whatever it takes,
Canadian ice-skater
Whatever it takes.

Dreams

In the safety of my dreams
we held each other

Gotcha!

Gotcha, ha, ha.
Found ya.
You think you can hide from me?
Me?
Don't you know who I am?
Don't you remember?

Found ya bitch on Facebook.
Fucked her page over.
Ha.
Saw her ugly face.
The wedding photo.
Bitch.
Her profile's hidden.
But Facebook made *changes*.
Yeah.
Changes.
I could see her groups.
Clicked and there you were.
Recognised ya straight away
that photo of the beach.
Ha.
Thought I wouldn't find you?
Wrong.
Raped your page.
Raped it.
Think you can hide from me?
Hide?
I'll show you.

See me

You don't
see me
you see
The ring
The child
The mother
The father
———dive under ———
I am
me
I am
more
I am
Yours

Do i know you?   Have we met?

If not in this world, then maybe, the next?
Or is it in another life that we've somehow
crossed paths
for we can't seem to stop talking
weaving

our

thoughts

laughing

piecing

together

creating & inspiring
inspiring   &   creating
The unveiling has been witnessed
You too see the dreariness
the despair, the dead ends
you too have indulged beyond that delicate line
only to find yourself
overthrown
I see the disease in your eyes
like oceans I long to drown in
The unease too does grip you
in fine-tuned melodies and guitar riffs
your voice projects the infection
just like I too, have written myself
underground

Take my hand:
we can elevate together
from misunderstood to magic
roaming free   un-catchable
and sleep will become
but a figment of the imagination
We can embrace the freak-show
the
shape   shift
like ghosts and apparitions
we can drift the streets
the disease lingering in our infected eyes
as we implode
within one another

What I am disgusted by

ONE
My own body
The plastic it's wrapped in

TWO
Questioning glances
The lights must be off
for humiliation to die
but still there is touch
your hand, tracing me
a reminder
that it's there
that flesh exists
that dirty bodies
mesh ungratified

THREE
My mind
Traditional
Entanglement
my legs crossed
our eyes
sewn shut
till it's time

Distance

In the forced distance between you and me
in the words we say, or do not say to each other
I can safely love you

Daylesford

Under the pretence of rekindling our love,
we pack our bags and journey, to lavender fields.
Between looming sunlit trees, layered in frost,
our childish whispers echo on bicycles made, for dreams.
We outlined maps, my love, our ambitions, circling the globe
to return to a little girl born to speak our language, in song.

Tired feet pamper in slippers whiter than bridal expectations,
robed, we drink the organic herbal teas, of our destruction.
Mineral springs bubble your sex, the sauna steams my skin,
masked, the treatments are thick, extracting the bacteria, between us.
Experienced hands knead our unexcited flesh, working at knots
refusing to release – our limbs have stiffened, to alienation.

The room is bigger than the size of my heart, smaller than yours,
two storeys of polished floors, stainless steel and leather comfort.
Without her, our half embraces dwindle to electronic entertainment,
our kisses, stamped on, postmarked for undiscovered destinations.
The candlelight over dinner flickers in the midnight woods,
our hopes fleeing to white witch predictions, and me
refusing to accept the cards, for what they really are.

We journey home. The seasons, have changed on us.
We freeze in the living room – your breathing panics,
scrambles to solve the Rubik's cube, peels the stickers.
Cloaked in pessimism, we mourn at the funeral,
our tears trapped, your hailstone admiration grating us

and then she comes, riding in on her sunshine smile
she points, asks if we can see the rainbow.
She brings wood, lights a fire with her kisses,
hugging us together she watches the ice drip away.

She asks us to take her, to lavender fields.

You love me

You love me completely,
unconditionally
but there's an entire

world

of me
you do not understand

and so being with you means
a part of me will always be

unloved

Forever

Only in our last breath
does forever vanish
into the mysticism
from which it sprang
and the wide-eyed thought
'Shit, that was my life!'
is suddenly, irrelevant
The sitting across
from o v e r w e i g h t
wedding vows
night and night again,
the forced romping
seems silly, really,
the parading diamonds
crystallise catastrophically
and exchanging it all
for the sweet k i s s
of unknown
isn't as scary as

that

last

b r e a t h

The person I knew, no longer exists

You are nowhere to be found.
Withered to dust, scattered by lovers
you howl with the night winds
above far torrential seas

You are nowhere to be found.

Eyes that shone like sunsets over lagoons
now overfilled with booze and bottles of wine,
you stood in your black coat in the corner
behind the crowd, so nobody could see you

But I see you

I saw you down the beer then the wine on stage
stumble over your lyrics, fumble with the pedals,
sweating your stress through each song
you held onto that guitar like it was
the only thing saving you, from death

I wanted to climb up there and convince you,
tell you that encased in my mind is your image,
the way you were before love stole you,
how you helped anyone who asked,
the way you smiled, that sort of half smile
with one edge on your lip upturned

but I didn't go up there
I didn't even talk to you
except for those few words
when I arrived and saw you
stumped in that corner, drinking
Your words were stilted
and when I turned away I knew
you were gone, forever

except up there on stage
where I could have sworn you glanced at me
and I caught a glimpse of the man who helped free me
but never even knew, he did

Mirror

MIRROR
REFLECT
I see you
in my
INFLECTION

Keeping to yourself

You say you want to keep to yourself
You're hurt, you're wounded
You want to keep our personal lives separate
And I, the fool, chased you with emails
Supported you, inflated your ego
All the while you ignored me
And neglected common courtesy
Wouldn't even say hello or goodbye
And I made excuses
That I should be there for you
Because I'm a nice person
And even though you can't give
I should give
Because I care
I really care
About you
You.
You.
Me.
Me.
Tonight I say no
I'm not coming to support you
Not sending you that email tomorrow
Not sending any more emails full stop
Tonight I've decided to keep to myself
I've decided I want to neglect common courtesy
And tact, and saying hello and goodbye
For the first time in my life I'm looking out for me
I don't want to be nice anymore
In fact, I want to be rude
Fuck you

Into my skin

The other night in your bedroom
while we were swapping ideas and music
just as we always do, there was a shift
and I absorbed your laughter, into my skin

When I went home, it took a few moments
to blink you to my reality:

I recall how we sat in the classroom of creativity
how I always took the seat furthest from you
never minded looking anyone but you in the eye
as we discussed Sylvia Plath and Bukowski
shared our poems and philosophies
how I'd sort of hoped you'd be around during the break
instead of disappearing into the library, of your mind

With the landscape of my heart now obliterated
I am no longer anyone's other than my own
With my feelings fenced in
I wait for the right moment
to reach for your hand,
and even if your fingers
should casually slip away
I don't fear the fall
for I know I'd safely land
on the cushion of our friendship

The other night in your bedroom
while we were swapping ideas and music

just as we always do, there was a shift
and I looked you directly in the eyes
I wanted you to come closer
all the way to my fence
for you're tall enough to peer over
but you just stood there and smiled
gracious and oblivious to my feelings
fenced apart by our friendship
and I was just there, nodding
absorbing your laughter
into my skin

Wog* guys

I am so over wog guys and their conformist attitudes
I want an Aussie* bloke without a drop of culture

We've only just met

We're sitting in a bar, drinking
and mid conversation, you grin at me
and I *know* what you're thinking
Emotions wide apart I'm ready
We've only just met, and already
I'm imagining you inside me
Radiating pleasure through me
You may think me too keen, a little intense
It doesn't matter
It doesn't matter who you are, really
My anonymous stranger
lay your hand on my bruised skin
let's get naked, under the covers of my mind

Dear stranger, kiss me me me kisssssssssssssss...

Davo

Yo Davo, where'd you go, Davo, where'd you go?
You've been on my mind, bro
but I gotta let you go
It's insane, I know
we don't even talk on the phone!
Waiting for your email from the unknown
Sometimes I wonder if you're out there all alone
if my messages are giving you some hope?

It's insane, I know
'cause we only met for a minute
just to exchange an eBay Soundwave ticket
you'd only moved to Melbourne the day before
but your shyness was so fine
a handshake that was sleek and sublime
and words soft enough to slow time
said we'd have coffee sometime on the fly
but then you had to go run off and hide

I know if we went out we would totally kill it
if you'd only just bloody meet me for a minute
yeah I got impatient and I told you to stick it
if I could wrestle my brain I'd certainly kick it

But I've really only got myself to blame
my emotions need to be seriously tamed
and for all I know you're playing some game
so I'd rather step back if it's all just the same
and soon you'll probably forget my name
I'll pass you on Brunnie streets, mistakenly turn away

and I'm wondering if this is all about control
and I just really need to heal my soul
Davo, you've been on my mind, bro
but seriously, seriously, I gotta let you go

Byebye Byebyeby

I think we're over

I think we're over before we began
But it's okay, I've been here many times before
I'm a complicated, neurotic poet with a kid
and you're a nice bloke, easily accessible
to the smart blonde down the road

Sorry for the trouble, good luck, all the best

Best friend

We travelled the world together
waltzed down the aisle together
created our daughter together
grew up together
Eternally one, our rings were inscribed

eternally one

My hand is still shaking as I hold the telephone
Your confession has pulled your blanket from under me
sensations of vomit pushing up me
my hands scrambling for words to hold onto
but there is nothing, nothing but tears
unknown's darkness gaping at me from below
and I know, the fall will last forever
'Don't you dare let her touch my daughter!' I shout.
'She's my daughter, she's my daughter,
she's my fucking daughter!'

Our separation slithers around my neck, the inhuman beast
mother, father, child, pulled apart by unnatural human factors
and now you're fucking our memory with this woman
her smell on our marital bed-sheets, raping my skin
manicured fingers tugging on the blankets of our love
our first touch woven into the threads
you're showering with her under our tears
in our house, our first home
the perfect white picket fence
sipping wine with her at our dinner table

where we taught our daughter how to eat,
cuddling with her on our couch
erasing the film of our lives together
'I haven't even moved all my stuff out,' I whispered.
'My wedding dress is still in the closet.'
I'm still in the closet.

When you went to work I packed up my stuff
dividing photos and cards,
crying and packing, packing and crying
my life bleeding from between my legs
one car load, back to my place and back again,
to Mum's to steal a kiss from our daughter
as she played with *Papou**,
watching Sleeping Beauty
she asks me to kiss her on the lips like the prince.

Presenting Mum with the wedding dress, the cardboard white coffin:

Crystallised Cynthia Briggs bridal gown
ivory silk, pulled up on one side with a flower,
purple tulle peeping through
the real me hidden under layers of antidepressants
I had a big fat Greek wedding and my parents
were the happiest parents in the world.

Telling Mum I'm going to sell it on eBay,
Mum, taking the coffin, saying the dress is hers

she paid for it, watching her take it away to her room
to crawl into, sleep in for all eternity
'My life is over,' she said.
'Me evales ston tafo.' You've put me in my grave.

When you came home from work
I still hadn't finished packing
You asked if I'd be long and I said
'Why, you expecting someone?'
And when you didn't answer I said
'Call her and tell her if she comes
into my house I'll kill *her and* I'll kill you.'
'It's not your house anymore,' you said.
I gave you back the keys.
'Don't worry,' I said,
'I'll be out of your hair soon
and then you can fuck on our bed.'

Best friends
We travelled the world together
waltzed down the aisle together
created our daughter together
grew up together
The night you rang to tell me
you said that we'd always love each other
But all I heard was the hammering of
the second-last nail in our pre-packaged love

The long awaited coffee date

When she steps out into the sinister night
she knows he wants more of her
so she leads him to the slim alley
down the bluestone where nobodies meet
their lips softly touching
hands slithering down skin
his tongue in her mouth now
lips wide, senses ablaze
and she knows she's not
going home, tonight

It's dark when they enter his place
quick to close the door
he nudges her flush to the wall
a swift movement of her skirt
he pulls down her underwear
locates her with his cock
and already he's inside
sighing in relief and ecstasy
this fuck months overdue
her palms hit the wall
he entwines his fingers, with hers

Slowly moving inside her
his lips and tongue on her ear
she removes a hand to touch herself
but his hand is quick to follow
he tells her to let *him* do it

but she pushes his hand away
because she's climbing now
and he'll only delay it, ruin it
fucking hell! he curses
why've you got to control everything?
Since the moment we met!
Why won't you just let me fuck you?
Why don't you just let **me** *fuck* **you**

Wedding photo

A large, framed, glass covered image
up on my parents' wall
never to be taken down
even though the people in it, are dead

I sit in my parents' formal living room alone
and I cry for them, because I know
I'll never see them again
even after I am gone myself

So much life in their eyes
among the gardens of paradise
I can't believe they're really gone
I want them back

Maybe things would have been different
if I could have had a chat to them
on their wedding day, or soon after.

Like they would have listened anyway,
so full of love and life.
Nothing would have stopped them
They were so young when they married,
just twenty-two, their whole lives ahead of them

Weddings are kind of funny
a rich, glossy photo encapsulating a union
But is it the love being captured or the myth?

And is every bride and groom
destined for the same death
that I, myself, have endured?

A large, framed, glass-covered image
up on my parents' wall
A stunning vision of my youth
Dead, out of reach
but never forgotten

Makeup

I better put my makeup on

or he might see

me

Push through

Living my life with my mobile beside me
waiting for the beep to inspire and surprise me
running to the crotch of every personable stranger
the grip of the thrill, the lust and the danger
down below in a hole excavated by myself alone
an email or an sms lifting me to places unknown
and my smile will be so perfect so fine
other single women will woo and delight
I've found him yes I have, the man of my dreams
together we will run to sunsets and dreams
hands entwined, bodies collide
slippery wet skin, oh so divine
the banging of the bedpost
against my patterned wall mind
banging and banging to thrills in the night
I want it to spill and your grip is so tight
memories ablaze and thoughts in a maze
I'll make the whole story up, you'll be so amazed
you won't have to speak, or say anything, really …
I'm an expert at this, you'll see soon, really …

Living my life with my mobile beside me
waiting for a beep to inspire and surprise me
the friend or the foe, the final fuck to free me
wanting their truth and their skin oh so near me
anything really to stop me from seeing

Idolising the emotionally unavailable
investing in guys that mirror my eyes

craving and lusting my very own demise
slashing the wrists of every relationship beside me
the weight of my thoughts crushing cement
clothes everywhere, dishes in the sink
my own little girl looking right down at me
do you need a mother, mummy?
do you need a mum?
not knowing how to stop myself
hunting the quick fixes
wanting to push through but not knowing
not knowing how to stop myself
push through
not knowing how to dance myself
push through
accept myself
push through
love myself
push through
nobody can make it better
push through
nobody can make it better
push through
nobody can **fix** it
push through
nobody can make it better
push through
stop chasing him down the street

push through

stop waiting for an email

push through

push through the pain

stop playing the game

push through

love you

push through

love you

I can't

Push through

Can't

Push

Love

Push

Breath

Push

You

Push Through

Attraction

I am attracted to emotionally unavailable men

because I am

emotionally unavailable

Love

I have dissected to the point of paralysis
I may be chemically reacting in your brain
but we are cut from the same blue-print of the species.
You may be looking at me like you know me
and you do: there are only two human types.
I am a clone of your antithesis.
On the other hand,
The electric guitar you're playing is euphoric
and you're screaming your lyrics down my throat
The kind of lovemaking I prefer,
one that doesn't involve
feminine latching and lunacy,
linger and lament.
There is no one of the opposite species
that fits perfectly to my clone
No miracle, no fairytales
It's just random criss-crossing
Procreating on the planet
This scientific experiment
of some higher energy
The experiment we call EARTH.

Worth

You weren't even worth writing a poem about

How to get a fuck

The only way to get a guy
Is to become one
Let's not pretend here
We, live in a MAN'S world

So get with the program

Keep your words to yourself,
your poems under your pillow
Forget fairytales and myths
Instead listen to
Bullet for my Valentine
loud, on the tram,
so you're silently screaming

Eye makeup should be dark
Challenge the fuckers
as they're checking you out
A short skirt, red lipstick
a long pair of boots
so you can stiletto their hearts

Step out into the night
Focus on the physical needs
Chase the fuck not the feel
Guys are experts
you can do it too

WAKE UP!

He doesn't want to know you
even if he asks about your life
He doesn't care about you
even if he shows you his garden
He doesn't think you're special
even if he plays the piano for you
or kisses your forehead,
or strokes your face
or holds you tight in the night
Don't believe him when he has no time
he's got three or four on the side

He just wants a fuck
to slide into your cunt
to ram you against the wall
pull your hair,
stare into your soul
Don't be fooled,
he just wants you to suck his cock
so he can feel like he's on top
Let him think he is
then take your stiletto and …

Don't fight it, don't deny it – this is life
We need to shield to survive
We have to hide our woman
Once he gets what he wants
he'll be gone in a drop
any sign of emotion

will set his feet in motion
Don't fight it, don't deny it
This is reality

Here, watch me take this knife
and plunge it into my chest
See the square I'm cutting?
See that?

There's my heart, beating

Here I will place it
on the kitchen bench
and with my bloodied hand
watch me create its coffin
a nail for every lover
every bastard I let inside
and ever so gently
and compassionately
I will lay you inside, my heart
I will lay you inside
and I will not cry
I will fight my tears

Hammer it shut
a nail for every time
I said I wouldn't and I did
hammer it again
and again and again

I will bury you in my chest, heart
mourn your loss, but I won't cry
I'm not crying, I'm not crying ...

See this needle?
Watch me sew my skin shut
a stitch for every falter
every time I believed another
saltwater sting falling from my eyes
feeling the agony of every stitch
in and out, in and out
the pull of the thread
so I can REMEMBER
that THIS is a MAN'S world
that they are all BASTARDS

Hey guy from across the bar, you like what you see?
You want to come over here and fuck with me?
You haven't got the balls to deal with me
Don't worry I'll only take what I need
You can penetrate my cunt
but I'll be fucked if I let any guy
ever again, penetrate my SOUL

Freedom

Give up on love and live freely!

When a relationship ends

When a relationship ends
it never does in a neat and tidy bow
and you have to let it go
even though there's unknown
Grieve its death
And accept
It's dead
Because in resisting
and sifting for hope
you block seeing others
You block your own path
You stop the pain passing through you
It's going to hurt like hell
but it must pass, like a virus
There is no stopping it
And you know you will be better
There is no point in rereading emails
or analysing, or sending him messages
When you're hurting so bad
you don't even know what you're feeling
the emotions are so intense they're bleeding
It must pass through you
Accept that it must pass
Don't fight it, let it pass
Close your eyes
Go to sleep
It will pass

You like to fuck
the darkness in me

When you hold me I tremble in your arms
but you just want to fuck the darkness in me
When I told you my friend died
I said the pain was so bad I needed sex
You came straight over, and you didn't speak
and I didn't want you to
You kissed me, and I cried in your mouth
Then you stopped, and we hugged, tight, and sighed
But then you just wanted to fuck the darkness in me
I wanted to be held, but you sent me straight to hell
where I want to be – where I, we, belong

We walk the fine line between pleasure and pain
friend or bastard it's all just the same
'I love sucking your cunt,' you said
'I love fucking you.'
You showed no mercy, your blunt, honest words
marking out the tall walls of whatever this is
'What are you?' you asked.
'Your friend,' I replied.
'What are you?'
'Your friend.'
Then you yanked at my hair. 'WHAT ARE YOU?'
'Your fuck buddy.'
'Good girl.'

You kissed me with an open mouth, with your tongue
You did things to me I never let anyone do
You pushed me into sucking your cock
I said, 'I don't do that,' but you didn't care
with my hair bunched in your hand
my vulnerability had the doors open wide
and you came inside
helping yourself to whatever you liked
ignoring things you did not

But don't you see, I did this all to me
I dictated how it should be
when you ended it with me
said we were too different
and that I wanted more
I should have let you walk out the door
but instead I said, teach me how to fuck without feeling
I need to learn, so I don't hurt, the same way again

But then my friend died
and my emotions were open wide
and I was telling you how much I love my friend
and you said, 'You love to love.'
'No,' I replied.
'You love to love.'
'No, because then you get hurt.'
'You love to love.'

And then I found myself saying I want us to be free
that I don't own you and you don't own me
that life is just about moments and we can just be
You can rest on my hand like a butterfly
and I'll watch you fly up to the sky …

'Then I'll treat you right,' you said,
'you just have to trust me.'
But what are we? I wanted to ask, but didn't
'What do you want me to do?' you asked.
'Hold me.'
'I'm holding you.'
'Hold me.'
'I'm holding you.'
'Stay with me.'
'No.'
'I need someone with me.'
'No, that's not what you want.'
'I want us to be friends.'
'It's not what you want.'

And you were right,
because the thought of holding your hand
petrifies me more than I can stand
and so, there was nothing more I could say
and I just let you be,
and you decided to fuck the darkness in me

And I liked it.

Her cunt

She resisted at first.
But he persisted, wrestled her to position
kissing her underwear right there, on the spot.
She thinks about it a lot. It was so hot.
Then he took off the cloth
and his tongue slid slowly to position
She thinks about it a lot, how the tip ran along the path
all the way to her clit, and worked there.
It was so fucking hot, his tongue lost the plot
Slowly at first, up and down, up, down and around
Yeah, faster … yeah, faster, oh, put your finger in
put your finger in there, so I'm completely self-aware
and I can feel your consuming stare
Yeah, yeah, yeah, yeah, yeah, yeah!

She thinks about him licking her a lot
She'd never liked it done before
She doesn't know why she likes it so much
There's an obvious lack of trust
But why does that even matter?
All she wants is her body to shatter
To feel ultimate pleasure drug-laced with pain
even though she never came that way

Yes, she was starting to play the game

You

Australian literature would suffer a great loss
if we stopped seeing each other

Diversification

Diversification is the name of the game I will play
I don't care if you made love to me
with George Michael serenading us
and you made me come so hard
I couldn't speak afterwards
I don't care that you gave me
three of the biggest orgasms of my life.
And I'd never tell you that
because then you'd have the upper hand.
Where's the next guy? I say
The next cutie, the next hottie I can fuck
so I can erase your thumbprints from my skin
I don't care if you said we come together
like a puzzle, where's the next guy? I say
Diversification is the name of the game
and I want to play, so let's play.

Puzzle

I know you're laughing at the title of this poem,
not all of you, just the one that this is about.
The night you said we fit together like a puzzle
when I came up to you at the bar, and we hugged,
before that, when the cabaret show was performing
I was watching you laugh at the show
and it made me feel good.
I like it when you're laughing,
because then you're not thinking.
I can never tell what you're thinking,
and that scares me, more than I want to admit.

In bed, later, our bodies interlocked like a jigsaw puzzle
You called me sweetheart, and you held my hand

even after I told you it scared me

Every time I see you it's better than the last
Just when I think it couldn't be any more intense
it is, and that scares me, more than I want to admit.
But I don't want anything serious
and you've made it clear that you don't
and so, I don't think it's a good idea
that we see each other anymore
and you'll never read or hear this poem

and you'll never know, why I ended it …

Your house

I want to kiss your eyes at sunrise
bathe with you in your bathtub
do all the things you won't allow
I want to kiss your eyes at sunrise
just like that one and only time
you gave yourself permission
to lose yourself in my arms
before your walls rose in defence
a maze of words miles wide

me at one extreme
you at the other
your heart at its heart

I doubt anyone has got that far.

In this darkness there is no negotiation
You do not run in search of me
You have survived effortlessly like this
and you will continue to do so
Am I a fool for walking in?
I don't know where I'm going
and sometimes I end up
right back where I started

This isn't a maze. It's a labyrinth.

I think about giving up
but your music lures me in
and then the words come like razors
incisions to my chest
Is this love or self harm?
It's hard to tell with us
Your ghostly kisses on my lips
and then I'm running along mirrors
and it's you I see, on the other side of me
Am I fool for searching for you?
But I knew with love and me
that this is the way it's got to be
and so, breathless, I run
towards the sunrise …

I don't know

Your kisses are the most surreal I have ever tasted
Your tongue, just the tip, soft in my mouth
But I don't know, I don't know
Am I just an instrument you're playing?
I don't know
Your eyes can engulf me
I think I like you but I don't know
When you leave after we make love
I sit with my torture
And all I want is to scrub
Your fingerprints from my skin
I don't know, I like you, but I don't know
Is this what it's supposed to be like?
I scramble for words that might mean
Something other than I just want to fuck you
I can't make sense of this
I just don't know
I don't know what I feel
What I want, what you want
Where this is going
If I'm heading for hills
Or a fatal car accident
I don't know
I'm scared
And I just don't know

Meeting a nice guy

You are so nice

and good

I'm afraid to touch you

Domination

I want it, no other way
'Fuck you. Did you hear me? F u c k   Y o u.
You will not survive.'
We're wrestling, just as we usually do, naked.
You're silent, but your eyes spill anger all over me.
I laugh at your lack of control over me.
'I won't suck your cock. Ha. Fuck you. Ha!'
You're strong, your arms are big and you're fucking strong.
I fight with everything I've got. Loser. You can't have me!
You get me on my back, straddle your legs around me.
'Fuck you. I won't suck you, you hear?'
I fight you with my arms, hit, but I'm laughing, I'm laughing.
You're not laughing. 'Suck my cock.'
I shake my head. You grab both my wrists.
You move forward, inch your body up mine.
You move your cock closer to my mouth, closer.
You get to my mouth. I turn my head. 'Fuck you.'
'Suck it.'
Momentary distraction from you and I'm on my stomach.
And we're fighting again. 'Fuck you!'
Fuck you for doing what you do to me.
You overpower and trap, flatten and compress me with your body.
Our arms lay side-by-side. Your cock is throbbing on my butt.
I can't move anything. I don't want to move anything, ever.
I can't see you but I know you're pissed.
You like your women submissive and I'm not that.
You take my ear into your mouth.
'Do you hear me? Fuck you.'

You don't speak. You hardly do.
You grab both wrists with one hand, tight.
You penetrate me with your other hand.
You're finger fucking me. It hurts. I like that it hurts
'It's too rough, fuck you, fuck you …'
You don't speak. You don't care.
You continue to do it

On and on and on ……

Domination.
Complete and utter submission.
And I want it, no other way.

Addictions

We have an addiction you and I

best we don't indulge too often

                                 or we might

                         lose

                       o

                             u

r

                       s

                                       e

l

           v

                     e

                     s

Gypsy

In our past lives, you and I were gypsies
our minds drifting through art and music
place to place, people to people
I think I was on my own though
stumbling, unable to cure loneliness
Our paths crossed briefly, I think
You played music for me
and I danced for you
You tried to teach me things
I couldn't get it right though
I think you moved on
because in this life
I was born, sad

A long time ago, I had a dream
that I was living the life of a gypsy,
free of repression and convention
A long time ago, I cried myself to sleep
and I dreamt of living like a gypsy
On my own palm, I read my future
and in it I saw today
as clear as the blue in your eyes
and so I left, in search of you

I met a wise woman from our past lives
You never got to meet her in this one
but she guided you in the last
When I met her I knew I knew her
She played me gypsy films and music

When I heard the music for the first time
your eyes flashed before me
but I hadn't met you yet
The music infiltrated my soul
and my eyes couldn't help but close
I fell in love on that day

The week before she died
I met you, and on the day of rebirth
we made love, ritualistically
passion from two lifetimes
wrestling for the wrongs of our past
neither of us backing down
resisting that we had come together
to do this all over again

You played music for me
and I danced for you
You want me to get it right this time
I can't seem to get it right this time
You want me to get it right this time
This is what I've always wanted
I would cry myself to sleep
and dream of this life
I hope I get it right this time
Because in the next life
I don't want to be born, sad

Loneliness

Loneliness lives in my living room

c
r
e
e
p
s

u
p

my

f
o
u
r

w
a
l
l
s

Red gypsy violinist

When I first heard your
gypsy band's music
I instantly fell in love
So I came to see you all

and there you were,

in your black corset tutu
I couldn't stop looking at you
Red ribbon flowing dark hair
seductress with that stare
you, with your red eye-makeup
your fish nets and soft, pale arms
who could possibly catch you?
or keep you in their arms?
fools that even try, fools
you tempt with your grin
seductress with those eyes
dancing them to delight
with your gypsy band
they can't help but stare
with your stage presence
commanding the attention
you rightfully deserve

Red gypsy violinist
what did you do to me?
solo you step off the stage
casually into the crowd
rest your chin to your violin

and they all watch, in awe
they want you to come to them
I wanted you to come to me
but who could catch you?
fools that even try, fools
you exist melodiously adrift
in the sorrowful lament
of your other half
You rest on its shoulder
and it cries for you
the tears you cannot
You live only for its sound
teasing with your smile
they all watched, in awe
but I cried for you
I cried for me
who could catch you?
you seductress, you
what did you do to me
red gypsy violinist?

I touched your hand later
and we exchanged words
I said you were beautiful
You said I was beautiful
Something stirred
Seductress, you, seductress
Fools they all are, fools
nobody can have you
you belong to your violin
what did you do to me
red gypsy violinist?
what did you do?

Me myself and love

I am the only one
that can love me
I don't know me
How can I love you?
I don't know me
I don't know you
I may like girls
I'm not sure
I'm the only one
who can find out
You're a great fuck
That's all you are
I can't like you
I don't even know
what the hell I like
but I masturbate
thinking of you
You can fuck me
better than I can
and you touch better
I am the only one
that can fuck me up
but I will learn me
so all of you let me be
except you, the kisser
you can come over
but you don't
validate me

I validate me
I won't wait for
your messages
to validate me
I am awesome
with or without them
I VALIDATE ME
Did you hear me?
I VALIDATE ME
Not you – ME
I will sit with me
alone with only me
that's all we all have
although others will
delude and deny
but I resist this
I will not fill my canyon
with co-dependency
I will fill it with me
getting to know me
standing alone with me
being strong with just me
and then I'll choose
the right man for me
You don't know me
but you want to
Better I do it first
You cannot cure

the sorrow in my stillness
only I can do that
I am the only one
that can sit with me
in a place for me
love that me
I am free to be me
to do whatever
to fuck whoever
as many as I want
whenever I want
I am free to explore
because I own me
you don't own me
nobody owns me
I am the only one
that can love me
I don't know me
you don't know me
but you can see me
because it serves me
Only me
Not you
ME

Your cock

I have never wanted to suck cock
because it's so wrong
and I'm a good Greek girl
meant to fuck only a husband
or sit tight-legged in church
But lately duty is irrelevant
because I'm obsessed with
the thought of your cock

I'll push you to the wall
tear down your pants
unleash your cock
til it's naked and
determined
before me

I'll stroke it, affectionately
your warm, wonderful flesh
and with my eyes
staring into yours, I'll whisper
I love the way you lick me
but I don't want you to hide
between my thighs
I want your cock
inside my mouth

I'll crouch to my knees
take you into my mouth
along with all my words
because I can fit a lot in there

and I will suck your cock, baby
from its start to its end
while stroking your balls
and then I'll lick you, I'll lick
rub my head, cheeks, lips
all over your stick
and with my hair everywhere
you'll knot your hand in there
pull my face back
to your cocoon

Or I'd love to sneak into your office
go under your desk as you protest
no, no, no, no
amongst all your paperwork
you'll scrunch the brief
that's been keeping you
away from me
inside your fist

Or maybe when we've stepped
back into your apartment after
dinner at your mother's house
chatting about work and the rest
and my hand somehow
makes its way down there
and I start saying *sshh*

But we're better wet
inside a shower
you, fucking my mouth

a handful of my hair again
controlling the thrust
and I want to feel your cock, baby
so don't be gentle, be rough

And at the climax
my hands will scramble
for my cunt because
I have to touch myself
so wet at what we're doing
you'll lose control
mumble, mutter
that if I don't stop
you are going to come
and you won't pleasure me
but I don't care
I won't stop
I just want
to suck you dry
hear you moan
yell out, shout out

cumcumcum

in my mouth
I want to

swallow

lick you dry
till we're calm again

Tranquilizer

I see you
Your eyes
Tranquilizer
We speak
In the sunlight
Your eyes
Bluer than clear skies
Tranquilizer
Our embrace
A melancholy blues song
Tranquilizer
Your touch, on my face
Unrequited love
My words
Evaporating in your gaze
I have nothing to say
You have nothing to say
Your smile
My smile
Look Lock
Catch up soon
Yeah, catch up soon
Walking, away
Tranquilizer
In the toilet cubicle
Sit there for an hour
Tranquilizer

Jazz song

We're a jazz song you and me
The piano, the sax, the violin
The blues, we're the blues
It's so good 'cause it's so sad
The scatting of our beat
here and there
don't know where
Before we make love
when we're kissing
I cry for the aftermath
The end of our song
I'm falling for you
But we're just jazzing
So good at the climax
We lose ourselves there
And then we're slowing
And my tears are falling
The last keys on the piano

And then we're over, again

We need to talk

We need to talk! We have to talk!
But then I see you, and I drop all my

w   o
       r   d
            s

until I remember them, when you leave me again

Player

Oh, you're so good
romance in your eyes
the element of surprise
will you take me out this week
possibly fall asleep, in my arms
Expert love-maker, you
It's an art-form
took years to perfect
You make the girls scream
make it feel like a dream

You're my playboy, my playboy

In your lonely little house
you play music for yourself
drink the loneliness away
and then you're out to play
Can't do relationships right now
for this, that and the other
or is it just a cover?
because one day, maybe you can
you see, it's all part of the plan
Keep them hoping,
Keep them moping
Give them love for three hours a fortnight
You love for three hours a fortnight
Love, for three hours a fortnight
Or however often it suits you

Three hours, you love for three hours
You love till there's an inkling of hurt
You love till it hurts
There's a little boy inside hurting
It's hurting, it *hurts*
Mum, quick get away
Mum – Dad – NO!
STOP! Please, just stop.

I'm so tired.

You vanish like a ghost
love evaporated into smoke
to the next lustful embrace
enjoying the last one's chase
Expert manipulator, you
out of contact, out of reach
but you've got lessons to teach
and you've always been upfront
no lies here, nothing to hide here
out of contact, out of reach
till you get that twitch
and then it's time to switch
and the next one's chasing now
and you're juggling emotions
to the point of exhaustion
but it doesn't matter
because here you're safe

and they don't love you
it's only because they can't have you
that's why they love you
and there's no way anyway
you're all frozen inside
that little boy went in there to hide
you see, he's not coming out
on the floor, in a corner, in a ball
he's crying, he's *crying*
And he's going to make the ones who love him pay
He says they've got to pay
He's not sure why but they've got to pay
For the past, for everything
He's going to make the ones who love him pay
So he can be sure, he has to be sure
Ice, his heart is ice
He's got to make them pay
so he can be certain
that the love is not self-serving
or convenient or charismatic
The little boy wants to know
so he can be sure, he has to be sure
that the love is as white
as the ice, that surrounds his soul

My words

A long time ago
when I was another person
and wore another face
I wrote short poems
to try to make sense
of myself:

1. with every wrong-footing
there is a right

2. two steps in the wrong path
equals one in the right

3. do not abuse yourself
for the blessing of a mistake

4. regret is a naïve word
– pray for mistakes

But that's all bullshit
when your actions hurt
people you care about

like I care about you

I've cried many tears in my life
all about things people have done to me
and my hardships, and my sad, sad life

I'm thirty-two years old
and tonight, for the first time
I'm crying tears for someone else
pain I inflicted with my words
oh, yes! my wonderful words!
my powerful, narcissistic words
oh, yes, I'm a poet
and don't I do it so well?
I can make the crowd
collapse into silence

like your silence

your hurt silence

I wanted to crawl into the phone
scoop up the pain in your chest
and bury it inside myself
not just the pain I caused
but the other pain too
the pain you hide from me

I heard it clearly for the first time, tonight

In my mind there is an image
of the person I dream to be
You make me want to be that person

Pity I had to hurt you to realise that
or to realise I care, so much more
than I thought, I was capable of

and so I write this poem
a pathetic attempt
to make it better
even though the decision you made
was actually what was best for me
and you proved you care
more than my self-sabotaging mind
allowed me to believe

so here's to my attempt
to making it better
here's to my bullshit words
it's all self-indulgent crap

My actions hurt people I care about

They can hurt people I care about

People I care about

like I care about you

Fantasy

you quickly strip off in standing
demand the removal of my attire
to which I whiningly obey
'but you're not fucking me,' I say
and we're fighting on the bed
you take hold of my breast, I slap you away
and you give me that look
explain you don't want any of that
that you want to fuck me properly
and you're playing with my clit
flicking my nipple with the other hand
star-gazing silently into my eyes
varying the pace and rhythm
till I'm coming all over your hand
and you're saying 'good girl, good girl'
then we're wrestling some more
and you're trying to get your raw cock in me
you forcefully spread my legs and penetrate
skin against skin, you demand words
I cry out my obsession for you
to which you whisper my name
tell me you're falling for me
ask me what we're doing
and I'm not sure, what we're doing
and you're fucking me slowly
keeping me tightly in place
you tease me with your cock
in a little, out a little

ask me if I'm liking it
ask me if I'm sure I'm liking it
because you can stop if I'm not liking it
and I assure you, I'm liking it! I'm liking it!
but you're not so sure, so you slow to a stop
and I'm begging you, but you don't care
Please fuck me! Fuck me!
you take a chunk of my hair, kiss my neck
and you're in deeper again, moving with your finger
and you're moaning you're gonna come
because I'm gonna come, we're gonna come
and you ask if I want it and I yell
'yes! more than anything I want you swimming inside me!'
and we're coming, we're coming, screaming names
yes, yes, fuck, yes, yes!

Fucked-up sexuality

It's the thrill of us that always leads to the kill of us
Like how I know you fuck other women
I think about it sometimes
you fucking or sucking, another chick's cunt
hard, turned on and charged
mumbling, teasing her, talking dirty
It's only when I see you kissing her lips
cupping her face, gently brushing her hair away
that reality reaches into my chest for the grab

I enjoy visualising you fucking others
when you're not around to fuck me
I know you're not going to stop fucking them
and maybe I don't want you to
because that might lead to
night-after-night mundane tv cuddles
and I'd rather add a little sugar to our sour seduction
I like that you fuck them, baby
I just don't want you to love them

The thrill of us always leads to the kill of us
Like how you won't fuck me anymore because I go nuts
spitfiring abusive smses across our stratosphere
when you haven't come round to fuck my next fix into me
and I'm obsessing about which bitch you've got your cock in tonight
But if you fucked me more regularly
this problem wouldn't have existed to begin with

Instead you kiss me, cuddle me
tell me I'm wonderful and intelligent
then disappear into another pussy
It twists my cunt, pains my heart
You unravel my brain then stitch it up again
this tantalising torture of yours

I want a man exactly like you
that society and my family would surely disapprove
but one that will keep my life interesting
for as long as my existence continues
I want you to make me feel alive, forever

On most days the thought of you
has me wet, all day and all night
I can masturbate ten times a day
just thinking of you tonguing my bud
and I never even liked that before you

I could easily find another guy to fuck
to cure my condition
yet I humbly stand beside you and wait
till you're ready to fuck me again
till you've forgiven my insanity
the thought that I'm saving myself for you
only compounding my delicious desire

It's not desperation that's my motivation
Maybe I am a sucker for pain
I may be unable to love without a game
Should I celebrate or be ashamed?
I am smart enough not to sign up for this
If I don't want it – but I do
Good Greek girl gone completely mad
Freud would just link it back to her controlling dad

But I don't want to get into all that
Maybe that's just made me who I am
And I should stop questioning and accept that
Maybe it's just being human, or just me
Or maybe, it's fucked up sexuality

Threesome

The night when you came to
see me perform,
after it was all over
and we were in amongst the crowd
you said you never felt so humiliated
and turned on at the same time
mentioned, like in passing conversation
that you once lived in a three-way relationship

and once again we

stopped and stared

you, with your provoking smirk
me, with my Greek eyes of astonishment

You never cease to petrify and enlighten

We parted that night with cuddles
a soft kiss to my neck
and I went home feeling
a little bit more normal

Unable to erase 'threesome' from my mind
I continually masturbate to my fantasy:

I am your woman, your queen
I am the only one in your heart
You place me before all others
who are merely pawns in our pleasure

One night we are out to dinner
You're holding my hand across the table
It's nice because, finally, we are each other's
I feel safe and secure in our relationship
and I know sex is sex but we have love

We are in love

Midway through our meals
you give me one of your smirks
'What is it?' I ask
You say you want me to meet the girl
you were fucking ten years ago,
the one you went on a swingers' rampage with
'What, the divorced one you've been chatting to from overseas?'
I know about her. You've told me about all of them
I'm always hungry to hear your stories,
eyes closed I breathe inside you as you speak
living the experiences I was never
strong enough to encounter

I could spend the rest of my life, writing about you

'Yeah. She's coming down for a holiday.'
'Oh yeah.'
'I showed her a photo of you. She thinks you're hot.'
I blush. 'Yeah?'
'Yep.'

In my fantasy, we all meet for dinner.
I like her – she's smart
interesting, naughty and a bit fucked
I study her beauty quietly.
I have never been with a woman
and you both know this.
I think I want to fuck her

Back at your apartment
it isn't long before you're kissing her
saying how much you've missed her
all while I'm lonely on
the other side of the room
but I'm trying hard
not to allow your affection for her
to seep into my heart, and I'm turned on
touching myself, afraid, embarrassed, confused
you both come over and take my hand

Stepping into the bedroom you transition,
uphold your role as bedroom director
demand the removal of all attire
She's thin, hasn't had babies
I wish I looked as good naked
You instruct us to both lie on our backs
then you're quickly inside her
but it's cold and I want cuddles
abandoned and on my own again
as is so dictated, in the reality of us

You cup my face, begin to kiss my lips
moan your pleasure into me
'How you feeling?'
I don't speak. I can't speak.
'I want words.'
I shake my head.
But then you say you won't fuck me
you'll come inside her
if I don't tell you how I feel
I roll away from you into the foetal position
You instantly withdraw from her
and are onto me, unravelling my body
so I'm on my back.

I can't look into your eyes.

You slide your finger inside me
'You're wet,' you say.
'I want you to fuck me, not her,' I say.
'But you're turned on,' you say. 'You like it.'
'It hurts that you're not fucking me!'
'How does this feel?' you ask
as you play, rub, manipulate my cunt
and that's when I come, most of my tears

You roll off me when you're done
sit up on your knees
'Kiss her,' you demand
but I'm searching for the bed-sheet
to cover my hesitation

until somehow I find myself beside her
with your hand pushing my face
into hers, and now I'm kissing her,
warm, womanly lips, and it's sweet
but then I can't breathe, I can't breathe
and I don't think I can do this anymore
I don't think I can so I roll away again
but you just get back to her
and I can hear you conversing
planning out what you're going to do to me
'I'll fuck her from behind,' you say
then you instruct her to lick my clit

'I don't want you to touch me,' I shout
push you away, push you both away
but you're quick to grab limbs
get me into your desired position
'Stop fighting. You like it'
I don't, but I do, but I don't say so
and so I surrender, my resistance

It feels so good having my man's arms
wrapped around me, protecting me, from myself
but I feel us, I feel us slipping into our darkness
and I don't know if I can go there again
but she knows, she knows how to lick me
'I don't want to do this!'
''Course you do. You've always wanted to do this.'
'I love you!'
You don't reciprocate. Instead you whisper

that after I come you are going to fuck her
'No,' I protest, but I'm moaning
and you ask how I feel
how I feel about that
that you don't want to come inside me
you would prefer to come inside her
and I say 'no, no, no'
but I'm coming, I'm coming at the thought
of you looking into my eyes
of seeing your pleasure, reflected in my pain
and you ask me if it will hurt me
but I don't respond so you demand words
you say 'I want words, I want words'
and I say, 'yes it will'
and you say, 'you like pain, it turns you on
you like pain, don't you, baby, you like it'
and I cry out 'yes, yes, yes', as I come

my agonising grief all over you

in the fantasy, and in, our reality

Silence

In my silence I see *beauty*

Starting to learn

It's scary but I don't think I've ever loved before
But I'm starting to learn what that might be like:

I give you space because that's what you need
even if I'm craving your presence like sunlight

I fight my inclination to possess you
even when you disappear and it hurts
I allow you the freedom to be yourself
and accept that this is how you cope with life

I'm there for you even when you're not there for me
not because you won't, because you can't
then courageously I battle my demons on my own

I don't use my sexuality to lure you to me
or to deflect insecurity and intimacy
I resist the temptation of our lovemaking
because getting to know your soul is sweeter

When I'm out-of-control I forcefully defuse it myself
by imagining you giving blood at the doctor's
so I'm not shouting but speaking to your essence

I want you to find peace and happiness
even if that means I lose you to someone else
I will kill the seed of paranoia that nags me
to define us – we are undefinable

and I'm not scouting for anyone better –
I'm just not interested right now

It's scary but I don't think I've ever loved before
But now statements like 'you've unblocked me'
are starting to make sense, and the fact that you exist
and think of me, makes life that little bit more awesome

Someone said to me:
You have to love the way you want to be loved
I'm not sure how long we'll last, but that's irrelevant
because finally, I think I'm starting to get it …

Temple

My body is a temple
You shall not cross
Unless you are worthy
Of my Communion

I have been angry
Desecrated my spirit
But I needed to do that
To arrive, here

Because:
I deserve happiness. I deserve love
I deserve someone who will give to me
Just as much, as I give to them

And I want it! I want love!
L   O   V   E
I want to embody ecstasy in side alleys
In dark corners, underneath stars
Everywhere, with my man
Explore our darkness and our light
And if you're not looking
For the same thing
M O V E   O N

And in the meantime:
Men can come, Men can go
I'm not looking
I'm happy on my own
And I will
Worship
My own
Temple

The queen

I am the queen, make no mistake
I am the queen of my being
I have complete and utter control
over my soul, and my emotions
I am the queen and I expect
the best, to treat myself with no less
than disciplined respect
Make no mistake, I need no man
to tell me what I can and can't do,
or how to be, or to satisfy me
The queen is capable of all that
On her own, she has her inner servants,
worshipping, taking care of her body,
feeding, breeding her mind, body, soul
The queen is happy on her own
A busy bee building her castle
She rules her own kingdom
And in matters of the heart
she falls in love, with herself
Hearts and hearts all round
And she won't lift a finger
for anyone other than the king
that will sit idly by her side
and won't run off and hide
Because she's got no time to play
Please would you just go away!
I can't be bothered with the game!
I just want to sleep, watch a DVD

I don't care if you're on your knees
with a hundred diamond rings
If you're not the king for me
then move on please
I have places to be
and a whole lot of time
to spend inside of me
And when her Greek parents
say they have found a man for her,
she tells them GO AWAY
God dammit, don't you see,
I don't need a man
I am a woman – W O M A N
I am the queen, of my being
Hear me, I am the queen

Glossary

Papou: Grandfather.

Aussie: Short for Australian but the term is typically used by a migrant or a person descending from migrants as a label for a person born in Australia descending from Anglo-Saxons.

Wog: In Australian English wog was originally a pejorative for Mediterranean migrants, though in recent decades its offensiveness has been defused in certain contexts by common usage in pop-culture produced by the descendants of Mediterranean migrants.

Acknowledgements

Thank you to my editor Les Zigomanis for being the tough editor I needed, who had every right to kill me during the editing of this book. Thanks to Sabina Hopfer and Christopher Lappas at Ilura Press for being my publishing family and for helping me give *Love and Fuck Poems* the facelift it deserved. To Amra Pajalic and Amy Bodossian for additional proofreading and editorial advice. Thank you to Kaliopi Malamas for makeup and hair, and for taking the photo for the cover. To all the teachers at RMIT TAFE Professional Writing and Editing, particularly Ania Walwicz for her inspiration and for encouraging me to think outside the box—this book would not exist without her.

Thank you to Leigh Hopkinson and Cam Hassard for being my much-needed extra arms and legs. To Christos Tsiolkas for on-going mentorship and support. And to anyone else who helped with this book and that I have forgotten to mention, I am truly grateful.

But mostly I want to thank my amazing family for their eternal support and for loving me 'no matter what μαλακίες come out of my mouth'.

And of course thank you to my princess. I do it all for you.

Credits

'Best friend', extract published in *Audio Overland II: Resistance* by Overland, 2013. It was also made into a film in 2014 and has screened at various film festivals, and it has been televised. It was shortlisted for the Australian Online Video Awards in 2017.

'Canadian ice-skater', published in *Blue Dog* (Vol 9, No 17) by Australian Poetry Centre, 2010.

'Daylesford', received a merit award in the Diasporic Literary Competition, 2011.

'Define me', translated into Czech and published in the journal *Partonyma,* issues 35-36, volume 9, 2020, University of Pardubice, and in *In Your Bedroom, Your Cats Are Sleeping: Anthology of the literary quarterly Partonyma.* A selection from the years 2012-2021, 2021, University of Pardubice.

'Gotcha!', published in *Recoil 3* by Mulla Mulla Press, 2012, and translated into Czech and published in the journal *Partonyma,* issues 35-36, volume 9, 2020, University of Pardubice.

'Makeup', translated into Czech and published in the journal *Partonyma,* issues 35-36, volume 9, 2020, University of Pardubice.

'Temple', made into a song by singer/songwriter Melpomeni, 2013.

'How to get a fuck', made into a film in 2014 and has screened at various film festivals, and it has been televised.

'Red gypsy violinist', published in *With Love From Queer-Kuir-Κουίρ (Postcolonial and Partitioned) Cyprus* by Right / Write the World, 2021.

'You like to fuck the darkness in me', published in *Fuck Poems: An Exceptional Anthology* by Lavender Ink., 2013.

'Your cock', published in *A Storytelling of Ravens: The Best of Little Raven Publishing 2011–2014;* and in *Little Raven One* e-book by Little Raven, 2012.

———

Many of the poems in this book form the basis of Koraly Dimitriadis's poetic monologue, KORALY: "I say the wrong things all the time".

About the author

Koraly Dimitriadis is a Cypriot-Australian writer and performer. She has had poems published in Polish, Czech, Greek and Greek-Cypriot, and her short stories, essays and poems have been published in *Southerly, Etchings, Overland, Unusual Works, Social Alternatives, Meanjin, Solid Air* (UQP), *Resilience* (Ultimo/Mascara), *Foyer* (UK) and others.

Koraly's poetry films have been shortlisted for prizes, screened at festivals and have been televised. Koraly has performed internationally, including at The Poetry Café (London) and The Bowery (New York). Koraly's poetic theatre monologue "I say the wrong things all the time" premiered at La Mama. Koraly performed in Outer Urban Projects's Poetic License (Melbourne Writers Festival, 45 Downstairs, Darebin Arts).

Koraly's essays/opinion articles have been published widely across Australia, including international publications *The Independent* (UK), *Shondaland, The Guardian, The Washington Post* and *Al Jazeera*. Koraly is a professional member of the American Society of Journalists and Authors.

For her fiction manuscript, *We Never Said Goodbye,* Koraly was awarded residencies at UNESCO City of Literature (Krakow), Wheeler Centre, Chantilly, HOANI (Cyprus) and Moreland Council.

Koraly holds a diploma in professional writing/editing (RMIT) and a double degree in accounting/computing (Monash). She has spoken on panels, run workshops, taught poetry at RMIT, and has been interviewed on television and radio including ABC's "The Conversation Hour with Jon Faine".

www.koralydimitriadis.com

Index

Printed in Great Britain
by Amazon